CUTTLEFISH

SAMANTHA BELL

Published in the United States of America by Cherry Lake Publishing
Ann Arbor, Michigan
www.cherrylakepublishing.com

Consultants: Dominique A. Didier, PhD, Associate Professor, Department of Biology, Millersville University;
Marla Conn, ReadAbility, Inc.
Book design: Sleeping Bear Press

Photo Credits: ©bikeriderlondon/Shutterstock Images, cover, 1, 17; ©Vilainecrevette/Shutterstock Images, 5; ©John A. Anderson/Shutterstock Images, 7; ©Richard Whitcombe/Shutterstock Images, 8; ©Paul Cowan/Thinkstock, 11; ©Dorling Kindersley/Thinkstock, 12; ©Rich Carey/Shutterstock Images, 15; ©Ethan Daniels/Shutterstock Images, 19, 24; ©Nippel/Shutterstock Images, 21; ©WILTSHIREYEOMAN/Shutterstock Images, 22; ©scubaluna/Shutterstock Images, 23; ©pnup65/Thinkstock, 27; ©LauraDin/Thinkstock, 29

Library of Congress Cataloging-in-Publication Data

Bell, Samantha, author.
Cuttlefish / by Samantha Bell.
    pages cm. — (Exploring our oceans)
  Summary: "Discover facts about cuttlefish, including physical features, habitat, life cycle, food,
  and threats to these ocean creatures. Photos, captions, and keywords supplement the narrative of
  this informational text"—Provided by publisher.
  Audience: Age 8-12.
  Audience: Grades 4 to 6.
  Includes bibliographical references and index.
  ISBN 978-1-63188-018-6 (hardcover)—ISBN 978-1-63188-061-2 (pbk.)— ISBN 978-1-63188-104-6 (pdf)—
  ISBN 978-1-63188-147-3 (ebook) 1. Cuttlefish—Juvenile literature. I. Title. II. Title: Cuttlefish. III.
  Series: 21st century skills library. Exploring our oceans.

  QL430.3.S47B45 2015
  594.58—dc23   2014005328

Cherry Lake Publishing would like to acknowledge the work of
The Partnership for 21st Century Skills. Please visit www.p21.org
for more information.

Printed in the United States of America
Corporate Graphics Inc.

ABOUT THE AUTHOR

Samantha Bell is a children's writer and illustrator living in South Carolina with her husband, four children, and lots of animals. She has illustrated a number of picture books, including some of her own. She has also written magazine articles, stories, and poems, as well as craft, activity, and wildlife books. She loves animals, being outdoors, and learning about all the amazing wonders of nature.

The author would like to thank Jean G. Bohl, PhD, Associate Professor, Department of Biology, Millersville University for her help while researching cuttlefish.

TABLE OF CONTENTS

ALIENS OF THE SEA

They have color-changing skin, three hearts, and bluish-green blood. Their **tentacles** pull other creatures for eating. No, they are not aliens from another planet. They are cuttlefish, and they are found in our very own oceans.

Cuttlefish are considered the most intelligent **invertebrates**. This brainy group includes the octopus, squid, and chambered nautilus. They are so smart that scientists have taught them to do new things. And they remember what they have learned.

[21ST CENTURY SKILLS LIBRARY]

Cuttlefish are some of the smartest animals in the ocean.

The word cephalopod means "head-footed." This is a good name for these creatures, since their feet are attached to their heads! The head of a cephalopod holds the brain and sensory organs. The feet include all of the arms and tentacles. Like other cephalopods, the body of the cuttlefish consists of a **mantle** that holds its organs.

There are about 120 known species of cuttlefish, and new ones are still being discovered. Cuttlefish can be as small as your thumb or as long as your arm. The Pfeffer's flamboyant cuttlefish is only about 2.5 inches long (6.3 cm). The giant Australian cuttlefish is one of the largest in the world. It can grow to be 2 feet (61 cm) long and weigh up to 11 pounds (5 kg).

Cuttlefish can be found in shallow water all over the world except around North and South America. Some cuttlefish live on the ocean's sandy floor. Others can be found in algae beds. Many live in the warm water of the reefs.

Cuttlefish come in many sizes and colors. They can even change color!

This cuttlefish is camouflaging itself in the sand on the ocean floor.

Some cuttlefish move from one area to another when the seasons change. They spend the summers close to shore. In the fall and winter, they move to deeper water. Cuttlefish have been found at depths of up to 650 feet (198 m).

Cuttlefish are active at different times of the day. Some species are diurnal, meaning they are active during the day. Some are nocturnal, or active at night. Other cuttlefish are only on the move at dawn and dusk. When cuttlefish aren't swimming and hunting, they hide under the sand.

The way the cuttlefish moves, communicates, and **camouflages** itself is almost unbelievable. But these incredible animals are very real.

GO DEEPER

THERE MAY BE MORE SPECIES OF CUTTLEFISH TO BE DISCOVERED. WHY DO YOU THINK THAT IS?

CHAPTER 2

A PERFECT DISGUISE

In many ways, cuttlefish are similar to their cousins. They look a lot like squids but with broader bodies. Also like a squid, a cuttlefish has a shell inside its body. This shell is called the cuttlebone. The cuttlebone has small chambers filled with gas and liquid. By changing these amounts, the cuttlefish can control its ability to float. It is able to hover over the sand like a submarine. When the cuttlefish dies, the cuttlebone often washes up on shore. Because it is made of calcium, it makes a healthy treat for pet birds. People collect and sell cuttlebones.

This cuttlebone has washed up on the beach.

The cuttlebone is located in the mantle. The mantle protects the inner organs and delicate gills. Water comes into the mantle and flows to the gills. Like other cephalopods, cuttlefish have three hearts. Two of the hearts pump blood to the large gills. The gills filter the oxygen, and it goes into the bloodstream. The third heart sends the blood through the rest of the body. The blood has a protein that contains copper. This makes the blood blue green in color. Our blood appears red because it contains iron.

BODY DIAGRAM

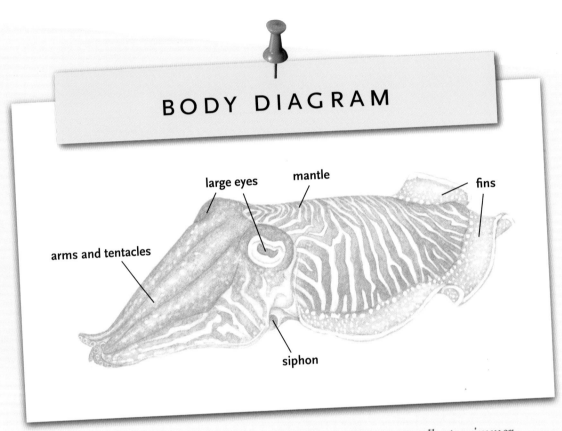

large eyes

mantle

fins

arms and tentacles

siphon

Long, flexible fins on the sides of the cuttlefish make it an excellent swimmer.

[21ST CENTURY SKILLS LIBRARY]

The fins of a cuttlefish are on either side of its mantle. They are as long as its body and move in smooth, wavelike motions. The fins allow the cuttlefish to swim in almost any direction. Cuttlefish can go forward, backward, and even in a circle. The fins also help the cuttlefish hover. With no bones or **cartilage**, the fins move more freely than fish fins.

Cephalopods are some of the ocean's best quick-change artists. They can change their color to match their surroundings almost instantly. Cuttlefish do this to send messages, attract mates, or hide from predators.

Though it may seem like magic, it's not. Cuttlefish just have amazing skin. Their skin contains 10 million to 20 million **chromatophores**. These are attached to tiny muscles. By flexing the muscles, the cuttlefish sends small dots of color to its skin. The cuttlefish combines these dots to create new colors and patterns that look exactly like the environment.

But this incredible skin can do even more. Cuttlefish can completely change their texture, too. They can make their skin look like rocks on the bottom of the ocean. They can make it look like floating seaweed. They not only blend in with their surroundings, they seem to disappear altogether. The cuttlefish is well camouflaged from predators.

Cuttlefish can't see colors, but their eyes are still highly developed. Cuttlefish eyes contain a lens, an iris, and a W-shaped pupil. This unusual pupil helps control the intensity of light that comes into the eye.

Chromatophores in a cuttlefish's skin help it change color and texture to match its surroundings.

LOOK AGAIN

LOOK CLOSELY AT THIS PHOTOGRAPH. IMAGINE YOU ARE THE PREDATOR LOOKING FOR PREY. CAN YOU SPOT THE CUTTLEFISH?

BIG EATERS

Cuttlefish grow quickly and are very active, so they use a lot of energy. This leaves them with a big appetite. They enjoy meals made up of mollusks, small crabs, shrimp, marine worms, fish, and even other cuttlefish.

Cuttlefish use their good eyesight to find prey. But they use another sense as well. Like other cephalopods, the cuttlefish has special **lateral** lines along its arms and head. These lines are like the "ears" of the cuttlefish. They are made up of thousands of hair cells that are sensitive to extremely small water movements.

Cuttlefish have eight arms and two tentacles to help them catch their prey.

Cuttlefish detect the tiniest movements made by their prey. In one study, scientists put cuttlefish in a dark tank. The cuttlefish couldn't see anything at all. But they still caught about 50 percent of the prey.

The cuttlefish doesn't have a typical mouth. Instead, it has a beak that looks a lot like a parrot's beak. Eight arms surround the beak. Each arm has four rows of suckers. Two tentacles are stored in pouches below the eyes. The tentacles are longer than the arms and are lined with suckers. The tips of the tentacles are also covered in suckers.

The cuttlefish disguises itself and moves in on its prey. In a whiplike motion, the cuttlefish grabs the animal with its tentacles. The arms bring the prey to the beak, and the tentacles go back into their pouches. If the animal has a hard shell, the cuttlefish uses its beak to crack it open. The cuttlefish also has a **radula** that helps it tear the food.

The cuttlefish does not always sneak up on its prey. It can often be seen holding two of its arms above its head and two out to the side. Some scientists believe the cuttlefish is catching vibrations made by prey.

Cuttlefish will also lure their prey by putting on an amazing show of color. Bands of color pass over the cuttlefish's skin. The colors move so fast that they seem to hypnotize the prey. While the prey is confused, the cuttlefish grabs it with its tentacles.

Cuttlefish have many ways of tricking prey.

LOOK AGAIN

LOOK CLOSELY AT THE POSITION OF THE CUTTLEFISH'S ARMS. HOW WOULD THIS LOOK TO ITS PREY?

Hundreds of Eggs

Cuttlefish have other reasons for changing their color. Their skin changes with their moods. An excited cuttlefish might go from a flashing yellow to a reddish orange. Then it might change to a blue-green color. It can even create two different patterns at the same time. It can show a dominant display to another male on one side of its body. At the same time, it can create a calm display on the other side to attract a female.

Depending on the species, cuttlefish are old enough to mate when they are between six months and two years old.

In the spring and summer, males and females move into warm, shallow water. The males fight over the best places for the females to deposit eggs. Some species look for a rock or shell. Other species find clumps of seaweed. Then the females come to the places they like the best.

A male cuttlefish sometimes changes color to match his mate.

The male cuttlefish often guards the female after mating.

Before the female mates, the male must win her. The males show the female their courtship displays. Bands of colors flash along their bodies. The larger cuttlefish with the better displays usually win. But there is hope for smaller cuttlefish. A small male can sometimes grab a female. Then he disguises himself to look like her. Sometimes the larger male does not notice that they are mating.

A female can mate with more than one male. Because of this, the males will often guard their female. They will fight other males to keep them away.

After mating, the female lays her eggs one by one. Some species lay white eggs under rocks or shells. Other species coat their eggs with black ink. Then they fasten them to seaweed. This makes the eggs harder for predators to see.

Cuttlefish will lay up to 500 eggs.

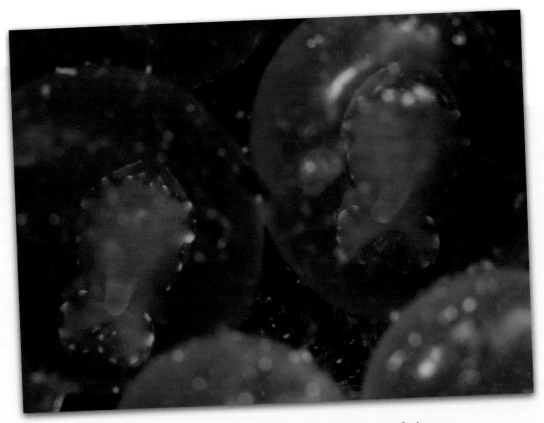
Cuttlefish babies must learn to swim and hunt on their own.

Depending on the species, the female will lay from 100 to 500 eggs over several days. But when she is finished, she leaves the eggs and dies. The males also die. The eggs must develop and hatch on their own.

Each cuttlefish egg is about as big as a dime. Even in the egg, cuttlefish embryos are able to learn. Some studies have shown that they are already using their eyes to watch different types of prey. When the cuttlefish hatch, they prefer to eat those animals.

Depending on the temperature of the water, cuttlefish babies hatch in 30 to 90 days. They look like their parents and soon start feeding on small prey. The young cuttlefish grow at different rates. In about a year, they also mate and die. The life span of a cuttlefish is only one to two years.

THINK ABOUT IT

MALE CUTTLEFISH ATTRACT FEMALES WITH THEIR COLORFUL SHOWS. CAN YOU THINK OF ANY OTHER ANIMALS THAT ATTRACT MATES THIS WAY?

CHAPTER 5

THE BEST DEFENSE

Cuttlefish catch a variety of prey, but sometimes they are the prey themselves. Whales, sharks, dolphins, seals, sea lions, seabirds, large fish, and other cuttlefish will eat them. A cuttlefish can camouflage itself to escape, but it has some other methods, too.

Sometimes the cuttlefish moves to avoid its enemies. First, it sucks water into its mantle through an opening near its head. When the pressure builds up, the cuttlefish pushes the water out. The force of the water shoots the cuttlefish in the opposite direction.

Cuttlefish have another way of avoiding danger. Like the squid and the octopus, the cuttlefish has an ink sac. When a predator comes too close, the cuttlefish sprays dark ink from the sac. This confuses the predator, allowing the cuttlefish to zip off the other way.

Cuttlefish can confuse prey by changing colors or spraying dark ink into the water.

Sometimes the cuttlefish squirts out the ink as large bubbles covered in **mucus**. These are about the same size as the cuttlefish. The cuttlefish uses them as decoys while it jets away. The ink contains a chemical. Some scientists believe the chemical may stop the predator's ability to smell and taste for a while. This gives the cuttlefish a better chance to escape.

Humans have been interested in cuttlefish for centuries. Since ancient Greek and Roman times, people have used their dark ink in dyes and paints. The ink is also used as a natural medicine. Sometimes people catch cuttlefish to eat. Others enjoy them as pets in their saltwater aquariums.

Cuttlefish are not on the **endangered** or threatened species lists. But like other marine animals, they are sometimes harmed by pollution and overfishing. By studying cuttlefish, we can learn how to help them. Then we can make sure that cuttlefish stay around for a long, long time.

Why do you think pollution is a threat to cuttlefish? What can you do to help?

LOOK AGAIN

LOOK CLOSELY AT THIS PHOTOGRAPH. DOES IT SHOW YOU SOMETHING ABOUT THE WAYS A CUTTLEFISH CAN DEFEND ITSELF?

THINK ABOUT IT

- Many people don't know much about cuttlefish. Besides reading about cuttlefish, what else can people do to find out more about them?

- Find a reliable Web site about cuttlefish. Compare the information on the Web site with the information in this book. Is it the same? If not, how is it different? Why do you think they are the same or different?

- There are many legends about giant cephalopods as sea monsters. If you didn't know about cuttlefish and you found one in the water, what story would you tell?

- Read chapter 2 again. What do you think is the chapter's main idea? What are three details the author uses to support this idea?

LEARN MORE

FURTHER READING

Coldiron, Deborah. *Cuttlefish*. Edina, MN: ABDO Publishing Co., 2009.

Sexton, Colleen. *Cuttlefish*. Minneapolis: Bellwether Media, 2010.

Strain Trueit, Trudi. *Octopuses, Squids, and Cuttlefish.* New York: Franklin Watts, 2002.

WEB SITES

Monterey Bay Aquarium: Splash Zone Coral Reef Animals
www.montereybayaquarium.org/efc/efc_splash/splash_animals_cuttlefish.aspx
Watch a video of two cuttlefish living in the Monterey Bay Aquarium.

National Geographic—Octopus and Squid: World's Deadliest: Hypnosis Attack
http://video.nationalgeographic.com/video/animals/invertebrates-animals
/octopus-and-squid/deadliest-cuttlefish-hypnosis
Watch a cuttlefish disguise itself, lull its prey into a trance, and snatch a crab.

PBS NOVA—Kings of Camouflage: Meet the Cuttlefish
www.youtube.com/watch?v=2x-8v1mxpR0
Watch the cuttlefish and listen to a scientist from the Marine Biological Laboratory in Woods Hole, Massachusetts.

GLOSSARY

camouflages (KAM-uh-flahj-iz) uses natural coloring as a disguise, enabling an animal to blend in with its surroundings

cartilage (KAHR-tuh-lij) flexible and strong tissue that gives shape

chromatophores (kro-MAH-tuh-forz) cells that contain pigment, or coloring

endangered (en-DAYN-jurd) at risk of becoming extinct or of dying out

invertebrates (in-VUR-tuh-brits) animals without a backbone

lateral (LAH-tuh-ruhl) coming from the side

mantle (MAN-tuhl) an outer or enclosing layer of tissue

mucus (MYOO-kuhs) slimy substance produced by an organism

radula (RA-juh-luh) a tonguelike structure with raspy teeth used for scraping food particles off a surface and drawing them into the mouth

tentacles (TEN-tuh-kuhlz) slender, flexible limbs in an animal, used for grasping or moving around, or containing sense organs

INDEX

[21ST CENTURY SKILLS LIBRARY]